Focused Equipment Improvement

for TPM Teams

SHOPFLOOR SERIES

Focused Equipment Improvement for TPM Teams

Edited by the Japan Institute of Plant Maintenance

CRC Press
Taylor & Francis Group
Boca Raton London New York

CRC Press is an imprint of the
Taylor & Francis Group, an informa business

Additional copies of this book are available from the publisher. Discounts are available for multiple copies through the Sales Department (800-394-6868). Address all other inquiries to:

Productivity Press
444 Park Avenue South, 7th floor
New York, NY 10016
Telephone: 212-686-5900
Telefax: 212-686-5411
E-mail: info@productivitypress.com

Book and cover design by William Stanton
Cover illustration by Gary Ragaglia, The Vision Group
Cartoons drawn and adapted by Gordon Ekdahl, Fineline Illustration
Page composition by The Marathon Group, Inc.
Printed and bound by Sheridanbooks, Inc. in the United States of America

Library of Congress Cataloging-in-Publication Data

Kobetsu kaizen no susumekata.
    Focused equipment improvement for TPM teams / edited by the Japan
Institute of Plant Maintenance : [translated by Karen Sandness].
        p.   cm. — (Shopfloor series)
    Includes bibliographical references (p.   ).
    ISBN 1-56327-081-1 (pbk.)
    1. Total productive maintenance.   I. Nihon Puranto Mentenansu
Kyōkai.   II. Title.   III. Series.
    TS192.K62   1997
    658.2'7—dc21   97-22741
                                                           CIP

09 08   10 9 8 7

Contents

Publisher's Message

Focused equipment improvement is one of the major pillars of total productive maintenance (TPM). In contrast with autonomous maintenance, which is intended to prevent accelerated deterioration of machine parts, focused improvement addresses specific equipment-related losses that reduce overall equipment effectiveness (OEE).

This method is called "focused" because it focuses on a particular type of loss. Also, it is intensively focused activity for which a TPM team may set aside an entire day or week. It is "improvement" because it goes beyond maintenance of basic operating conditions to directly improve the equipment performance or capability. Focused improvement gives teams tools that free processes from chronic losses and the effects of design weaknesses.

While autonomous maintenance is carried out by production workers on a daily basis, focused improvement is a periodic cross-functional project team activity. Production workers, maintenance technicians, engineers, and their managers bring together their expertise and unique perspectives in a common problem-solving effort.

TPM teams engaging in focused improvement often encounter recurring problems in machine performance. Chapter 1 reviews the basic principles of P-M analysis, a method designed to deal with chronic problems with complex causes, especially in the area of quality. (For more on P-M analysis, see "Additional Resources" at the end of the book.)

Chapters 2 through 6 of the book take on five of the six major equipment-related losses, describing basic principles and sharing examples for dealing with them. Chapter 2 focuses on breakdowns and an approach for preventing them. In Chapter 3, readers will gain tips on shortening changeover adjustment time by improving equipment precision and using standard, easily established numeric settings.

Chapter 4 examines minor stoppages, those nagging snags in automated and transfer lines that can defeat the benefits of automation. Chapter 5 goes after speed loss, reviewing ways to identify and analyze it. Chapter 6 focuses on equipment improvement methods for ensuring defect-free product quality. A list of additional resources rounds out the material.

This book is specifically intended to introduce focused improvement theories and methods to a shopfloor audience, with cartoons, dialogues, and examples to give readers a flavor of this approach. The material from which it was developed was prepared by contributors from Nachi-Fujikoshi Corporation, a world class machining company that has won the PM Prize for excellence in TPM. The basic principles in each chapter are applicable to most fabrication and assembly industries, but the examples are geared specifically to machining and will be most useful to facilities involved in high-precision machining of metals.

We would like to express appreciation to the Japan Institute of Plant Maintenance for permitting us to publish this English edition of their original book, with special thanks to Kunio

Shirose of JIPM and the contributors from Nachi–Fujikoshi Corporation for their development of the original material.

Thanks also to Karen Sandness for translation of this material; to Gordon Ekdahl/Fineline Illustration for cartoon production; to Sheryl Rose for copyediting; to The Marathon Group, Inc. for page composition; to Bill Stanton for the design; and to Gary Ragaglia for the cover illustration. Special thanks to Derrell Denny and Russ Phillips of the Warn Industries TPM team for reviewing the manuscript.

Many people within Productivity helped create this book. Thanks to Diane Asay, editor in chief; Karen Jones, senior development editor; Connie Dyer, TPM development director for Productivity, Inc.; Susan Swanson, prepress editor; Carla Refojo, cover production; and Jessica Letteney, prepress manager.

Preface

This book is a compendium of material that first appeared in the *Focused Improvement for Operators Series*, a set of pamphlets published by Nachi-Fujikoshi Corporation for their workers. The series itself was popular from the beginning, but many other companies asked us to bring the materials together into one volume, as we did with *Autonomous Maintenance for Operators*. In response to these requests, we brought all the information together in one book in the hope that even more people will read and benefit from it.

The series that this book came from was put together by the staff members who had played major roles in implementing TPM at Nachi-Fujikoshi Corporation, which received the PM Distinguished Plant Prize in 1984. Here is a brief summary of the contents.

The first chapter, "Thinking Systematically," offers a simple introduction to P-M analysis, a basic methodology used in focused improvement. Chapter 2 presents specific hints for breakdown analysis, while Chapter 3 provides basic ideas for simplifying and shortening setups. The next two chapters deal with performance losses: Chapter 4 covers minor stoppages, and Chapter 5 covers speed loss. Chapter 6 explains the basic concepts of using your equipment to "build in" quality.

This book is built around a number of specific examples from the experiences at Fujikoshi, a machine tool company. The examples relate to machining processes and may not be entirely applicable to other industries.

In the past few years, more companies than ever before have developed TPM reference books aimed at various departments and all levels of employees. I hope that this book will play an important role in promoting focused improvement within manufacturing companies.

Finally, I would like to express my deep appreciation to Nachi-Fujikoshi Corporation for graciously allowing us to adapt this material.

Kunio Shirose
Executive Vice President
Assistant Director of TPM Promotion Operations
Japan Institute of Plant Maintenance

Contributors

Chief Editor: Kunio Shirose, Executive Vice President, Assistant Director of TPM Operations, Japan Institute of Plant Maintenance

Yoshifumi Kimura, Engineer, TQC Promotion Office, Nachi-Fujikoshi Corporation

Eiichi Hongou, TPM Promotion Deputy Manager, Nachi-Fujikoshi Corporation

Mitsugu Kaneda, Engineer, TQC Promotion Office, Nachi-Fujikoshi Corporation

Masahiro Morimoto, Engineer, TQC Promotion Office, Nachi-Fujikoshi Corporation

Yasuhide Ueno, Engineer, TQC Promotion Office, Nachi-Fujikoshi Corporation

Ryôei Yoshida, Manager, TQC Promotion Office, Nachi-Fujikoshi Corporation

Thinking Systematically

CHAPTER OVERVIEW

What It Means to Think Systematically

Every company that makes products with machines ought to have *zero* breakdowns and *zero* defects. But in real life, you probably look at a defect rate of 0.5 to 1.0 percent and think, "That's just the way things are." If breakdowns occur every three months or so, you probably think, "It's natural for equipment to break down once in a while or produce some defective products, no matter what."

Nevertheless, many workplaces have achieved zero defects and zero breakdowns, thanks to employees who have developed the habit of thinking systematically.

The heart of thinking systematically about problems is the process of asking "why?" over and over again until we understand the situation and its causes. As we aim for zero breakdowns and zero defects, let's look at some points to remember when we ask "why?"

This chapter introduces key steps of P-M analysis, a systematic thinking approach that can be used during focused improvement to resolve recurring and multifactor problems.*

*For more on P-M analysis, see the Publisher's Message (p. ix) and Additional Resources (p. 121).

Form a Clear Picture of What's Going On

Why don't our improvements yield results that last?

In most manufacturing plants, people usually don't notice problems until they show up in the results: equipment that breaks down a lot, a process that yields rejects, or production that just won't go according to plan. In most cases, we try to think of ways to deal with these situations *after* we've noticed them. And in most cases, we then fall back on past experience, guesswork, or "quick and dirty" solutions. As a result, our efforts at improvement flounder aimlessly.

To begin thinking systematically about the problem, the very first step is to form a clear picture of the situation that needs improvement.

It's important to take a good look at the situation, narrowing down our view to the specific problem that occurs. We move from "This process yields a lot of defects" to "Most of the defects happen in grinding the rims," to "The biggest problem in grinding the rims is defects in the outer diameter dimensions," to "The finished dimensions we're getting from this cylindrical grinder vary by as much as 50 microns," to "We won't be able to reduce defects until we are confident that the output of this equipment doesn't vary by more than 20 microns."

Improvement begins with looking at problem areas *in terms of their physical causes.*

4

Thinking Systematically about the Problem

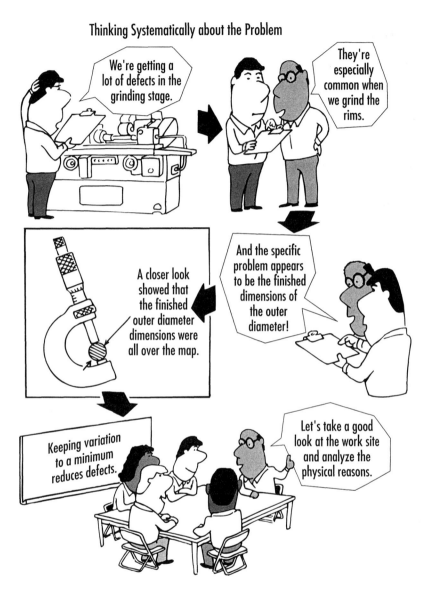

5

Explain the Situation in Physical Terms

The biggest trap to avoid when we're trying to gain a clear picture of the problem and implement improvements is *jumping to conclusions about the causes based on our past experience.*

To continue with the previous example, experience may tell us that when a cylindrical grinder produces finished dimensions that vary widely, the cause is usually sliding surfaces of the grindstone that are rubbing together or a dressing diamond that needs adjustment. If we stop there, however, we may overlook other causes contributing to the malfunction. This is why we look carefully at how the defect or failure occurred—in physical terms.

Remember that equipment failures arise from a chain of causes that violate the physical principles and standards that govern a process. To track down the causes of a malfunction, we must first understand how the process functions to produce a normal result and then explain the malfunction in physical terms: How do machine parts or process conditions interact? How did their interaction change to produce the abnormal result? For example, after studying the process and its standards, we may observe that varying dimensions result from random changes in the relative positions of the workpiece and the grindstone during machining.

This physical analysis is an important early step in thinking systematically, and once we've taken it, everyone grappling with the problem can talk about it in the same terms.

Think about the Conditions
Influencing the Problem

When our analysis of the situation gets bogged down, it is usually because we don't fully understand how the various mechanisms of our equipment influence quality.

The equipment is made up of units, the units of assemblies, and the assemblies of structural components. Do we understand the role each mechanism plays in turning out products? If we don't, an effective way to discover the relation between our equipment and quality is to clarify and document what we already know, research what we don't know by studying users' manuals, and then map it out in a simple structural diagram.

Looking further to understand what can cause a mechanism to malfunction leads us to consider more closely *the conditions surrounding the problem*.

For example, it's helpful to know that when a grinder produces variable finished dimensions, it could be caused by variation in the amount of dressing, the amount of grindstone in-feed compensation, or the grinding cycle time; by changes in the mounting conditions of the materials; or by defects carried over from the previous process.

Think about Connections with the 4Ms

Sometimes we can't seem to reach the real cause of a problem, even after we have adjusted the functions and structures of our equipment and understood their relation to product quality. This can happen when we ignore minor problems that come to light during our investigation. We assume that things so small couldn't possibly influence quality, and we do not include them on our list of possible causes.

At this point we need to review the relationships between the product defect and various factors that may influence it, sometimes referred to as the 4Ms:

1. Machines: equipment function and precision

2. Men (people): level of human skills, behaviors, and adherence to standards

3. Materials: quality of incoming parts or materials

4. Methods: appropriateness of operating and inspection methods and standards

Avoid jumping to conclusions about the possible effects of any factor; instead, note down and review all 4Ms to make sure you have considered all factors. Make sure that you understand the operating standards and principles that govern the factors you identify. Then ask whether each factor is in fact influencing the malfunction, e.g., were all processing conditions within specified ranges?

What reasons can you think of for malfunctions in the mechanism that corrects the dimensions? List everything that comes to mind.

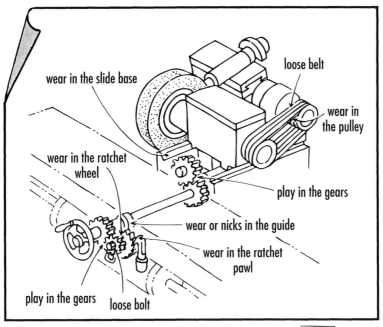

Hints for Inspection and Restoration

If we make improvements only in relation to the items that first appear to affect the problem, we won't get the results we expect. With this attitude, in fact, we're not really aiming for zero equipment malfunctions.

In the previous step, we wrote down all the possible causes of chronic malfunction. To eliminate these malfunctions, we must now look at each cause in light of the actual situation in our plant.

Since it would take a long time to inspect each component individually, we group the items to be checked together and try to look at them on a broader scale. Then, if there's a discrepancy between the results of our inspection and the standard operating conditions, we can isolate the abnormal component parts and look at them one by one, restoring the equipment to its proper conditions.

To achieve zero breakdowns and zero defects in the workplace, we must eliminate each abnormality one by one, so that we end up with zero abnormalities.

Hints for Maintenance Management

When we can't maintain our improved results, it's usually because we've omitted a maintenance item or because our standards are too lax. People may feel that there are too many items to monitor, or that it takes too long to check every item one by one.

A hint for dealing with this problem is to group items for maintenance management, just as we grouped items for inspection in the previous step. Another hint is to use our knowledge about each maintenance item to inform our operation of the equipment so that we maintain the standards strictly.

In that way, we can monitor any changes in the status of an inspection item during operation, and except for occasions when we have to take preventive measures to avoid a malfunction, there's no reason to worry about maintaining the results.

If we think systematically, carefully determine the conditions we need to control, and monitor them with utmost care, then we will truly be acting systematically.

Improvement Example—Cylindrical Grinder

1. Get a grasp of the actual situation

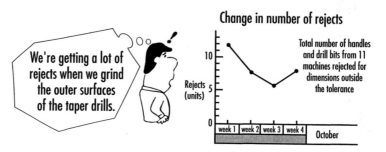

2. Specify the problem

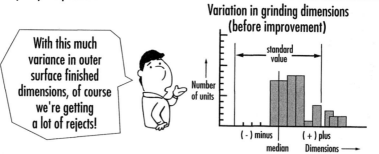

3. Conduct a physical analysis

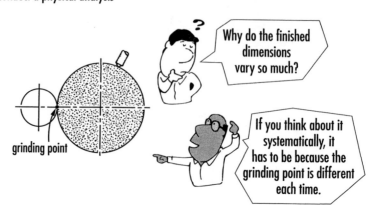

4. Consider conditions that can vary

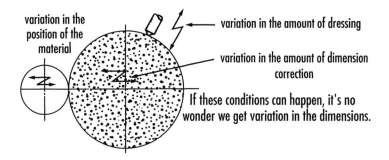

variation in the position of the material

variation in the amount of dressing

variation in the amount of dimension correction

If these conditions can happen, it's no wonder we get variation in the dimensions.

5. Consider the problem in relation to possible casual factors

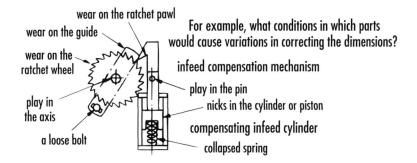

wear on the ratchet pawl

wear on the guide

wear on the ratchet wheel

play in the axis

a loose bolt

For example, what conditions in which parts would cause variations in correcting the dimensions?

infeed compensation mechanism

play in the pin

nicks in the cylinder or piston

compensating infeed cylinder

collapsed spring

17

6. Hints for inspection and restoration

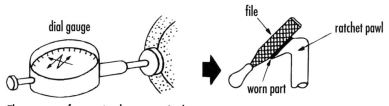

dial gauge

file

ratchet pawl

worn part

The amount of correction keeps varying!

The ratchet pawl is worn!

Fix anything that's abnormal, and fix it right.

7. Check the results

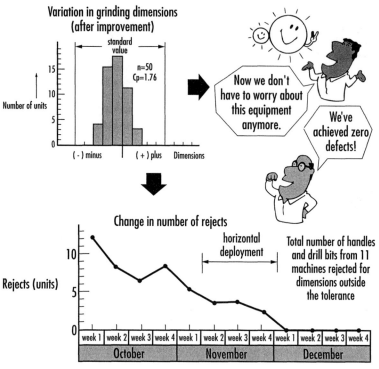

Variation in grinding dimensions (after improvement)

standard value

n=50
Cp=1.76

Number of units

(-) minus   (+) plus   Dimensions

Now we don't have to worry about this equipment anymore.

We've achieved zero defects!

Change in number of rejects

horizontal deployment

Total number of handles and drill bits from 11 machines rejected for dimensions outside the tolerance

Rejects (units)

| week 1 | week 2 | week 3 | week 4 | week 1 | week 2 | week 3 | week 4 | week 1 | week 2 | week 3 | week 4 |

October   November   December

8. Maintain the improvement

We won't let the same malfunction happen twice!

Equipment status

Great, there's nothing to worry about!

CHAPTER SUMMARY

Workplaces can achieve zero defects and zero breakdowns when employees develop the habit of thinking systematically about equipment problems. The heart of thinking systematically about problems is the process of asking "why?" over and over again until we understand the situation and its causes. This chapter introduces key steps of P-M analysis, a systematic thinking approach that can be used during focused improvement to resolve recurring and multifactor problems.

The first step in systematic thinking is to form a clear picture of the actual situation. Once we've identified the problem, it's important not to jump to a conclusion about its cause—we may be overlooking other factors that contribute to the problem. This is why we look carefully at how the defect or failure occurred—in physical terms.

Equipment-related problems arise from a chain of causes that violate the principles and standards of the process. We have to understand how the process functions to produce a normal result and how the interaction of machine parts or process conditions changed to produce the abnormal result.

Once we understand what happens physically during a particular problem, we can look more closely at specific conditions that influence the problem. To make sure we consider all the potential factors, we can refer to the 4Ms as a brief checklist:

- Machines: equipment function and precision

- Men (people): level of human skills, behaviors, and adherence to standards

• Materials: quality of incoming parts or materials

• Methods: appropriateness of operating and inspection methods and standards

In the previous step, we wrote down all the possible causes of chronic malfunction. To eliminate these malfunctions, we must now look at each cause in light of the actual situation in our plant. Since it would take a long time to inspect each component individually, we group the items to be checked together and try to look at them on a broader scale.

When we can't maintain our improved results, it's usually because we've omitted a maintenance item or because our standards are too lax. People may feel that there are too many items to monitor, or that it takes too long to check every item one by one.

A hint for dealing with this problem is to group items for maintenance management, as we grouped inspection items in the previous step. We can also use our knowledge about each maintenance item to inform our operation of the equipment so that we maintain the standards strictly.

Learning from Breakdowns

CHAPTER 2

22

Breakdown Summary Chart (January 12 – March 11)

No.	Date	Line name	Machine	Down-time (min)	What happened	Defective parts	Causes	
							defects in parts	human error
1	1/12	Outer 4	F-118A	30	slow table speed	flow control valve	clogged with debris due to dirt in the hydraulic oil	not paying attention to dirt in the hydraulic oil
2	1/13	Outer 9	NHO-271	60	poor action of pressing roller	limit switch	insulation defect due to incursion of processing oil	not noticing the leakage of processing oil into the interior
3	1/14	Outer 5	NAN-110	45	abnormal noise	bearing	wear due to leakage of processing oil	same as above

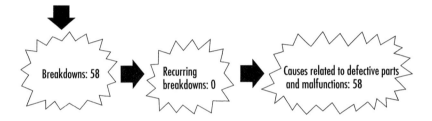

Breakdowns: 58 → Recurring breakdowns: 0 → Causes related to defective parts and malfunctions: 58

What Do We Mean by "Breakdown"?

The chart on this page describes a few of the 58 breakdowns that occurred in a certain plant during a three-month period, as well as the parts involved and the causes. A close review of the entire chart revealed that the same part never broke down twice due to the same cause; rather the breakdowns occurred in several parts due to several causes.

This chart shows a typical pattern in which breakdowns arise from any number of abnormalities in the equipment, sometimes from a single defect. Sometimes a single abnormality may cause the breakdown, but many breakdowns result from the cumulative effects of several abnormalities. For this reason, dealing with breakdowns is more than a matter of fixing problems one by one as they are noticed. Unless we deal with *all* the abnormalities at once and restore the equipment to its proper state, we won't obtain the results we want.

Breakdowns According to Cause

Period: January–March

N = 58

Break-downs

24

8

6

6

5

3

2

1

3

cleaning, lubricating, and tightening errors

fluid contamin-ation

worn parts

loss of precision

retooling errors

misoperation

repair errors

design problems

other

100%

50

Failure to notice these points

What Are the Real Causes of Breakdowns?

The Pareto chart on this page displays the real causes of the 58 breakdowns from the example on the previous page. Some problems were unavoidable, but almost all the breakdowns related to things that could have been prevented: contamination, running out of lubricant, loose nuts or bolts, neglect of worn parts, or mistakes in operation, changeover, retooling, or repairs.

As we think about these causes, we realize that equipment doesn't just break down by itself for no reason—and the reasons for breakdowns have a lot to do with how we operate and care for our equipment.

The Operator's Role in Routine Maintenance

25

Discovering all the abnormalities and using the equipment correctly are tasks too big for just the maintenance department. Eliminating breakdowns requires the help of everyone in the plant. Operators have a special role because we are most familiar with the equipment we use every day.

In TPM, operators clean their machines and check them for parts that are loose or have too much play. During operation, we watch for abnormal temperature, vibration, sound, and action; keep the lubrication supply at proper levels; and run or retool the equipment according to proper procedures. This is what we call autonomous maintenance.*

To make sure our machines will do what we need them to, we treat them with tender loving care.

*To learn more about autonomous maintenance, see Additional Resources on p. 121.

A Procedure for Achieving Zero Breakdowns

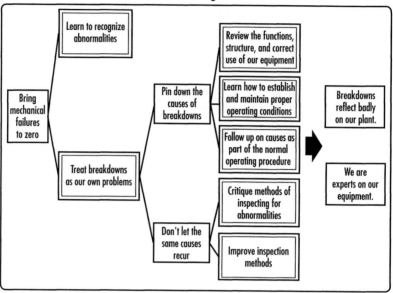

Learn from Breakdowns

The operator's routine daily maintenance activities are a critical first step in eliminating breakdowns, but by themselves they aren't enough. TPM teams need to analyze the breakdowns that occur from day to day, pin down the exact cause of each one, and determine how to adjust routine maintenance activities so causes are detected and treated early. In real life, however, breakdowns are usually analyzed in an aimless and haphazard way.

The chart on this page suggests a systematic approach teams can use for analyzing and learning from breakdowns. The rest of this chapter describes these steps in more detail and gives examples of breakdown analysis.

Tag abnormalities

One-point lesson

1. Basic knowledge about equipment maintenance
2. Actual examples of breakdowns and defects
3. Examples of equipment improvements

Use one-point lessons

Learn to Recognize Abnormalities

Operators need to understand how their equipment works and know their roles as makers of products before they can recognize or understand equipment abnormalities. TPM teams can use the following approaches to help everyone understand equipment systems and trouble points.

1. *Use actual objects to demonstrate.* Choosing a piece of equipment as a model, the team leader (or another person who understands the machine) inspects for abnormalities ahead of time, attaches tags to the trouble spots, and uses the tagged areas as visual aids.

2. *Teach the principle in a one-point lesson.*

   • Basic knowledge about nuts, bolts, belts, lubrication, oil pressure, and other maintenance items

   • Actual examples of breakdowns and defects that occurred when malfunctions and abnormalities were overlooked

Treat Breakdowns as Our Own Problems

Team leader: The circuit breaker for the conveyor belt motor kept tripping, so we had the motor replaced.

28

Section manager: I wonder whether the current was too high. What was the amperage?

Team leader: I don't know—I had the electrician come and look at it, and he said we ought to replace the motor. After all, he's the expert.

Section manager: That's true, but the team may not be able to keep this malfunction from happening again unless you investigate and understand it yourselves.

Team leader: Well, okay—but we'll have to learn more about electricity.

TPM teams should learn the basics about all their equipment subsystems, e.g., fastener, electrical, hydraulic, pneumatic, and drive systems. In that way they can recognize and actively prevent more problems.

Really know the functions and structure
of your equipment.

Structural diagram

Learn about the Functions, Structure, and Correct Use of Equipment

Team member A: There was chattering on the grinding surfaces, and when I looked at the quill that attaches the grindstone to its spindle, it was vibrating too much, so I replaced the quill with a new one. Everything should be fine now.

Team member B: I suppose the quill may have been part of the problem, but are you sure it was the only problem? If we're talking about the spindle drive, shouldn't we be looking at the belt or the overdrive?

Team member A: Well, uh, the drive portion is inside the cover, so I didn't look at it.

In fact, changes in the tension or inclination of the drive belt can cause chattering on the grinding surface, and so can vibration in the overdrive. If we don't learn the functions, structure, and correct use of our equipment, we usually end up with an incomplete analysis of breakdowns.

29

Establish and Maintain Proper Operating Conditions

Unless we understand the proper operating state of our equipment and its components—the way they are when everything is in perfect working order—we won't be able to analyze the reasons why a breakdown has occurred.

The two charts on this page show sample inspection checklists that describe the proper conditions for a limit switch and an oil pressure pump.

Sample Inspection Checklists

Limit Switch	Oil Pressure Pump
Check Items	**Check Items**
1. Correct stop position	1. Discharge pressure set correctly
2. Correct limit switch position	2. Correct amount of oil in tank
3. No play in pin	3. Strainer not clogged by debris
4. Roller on track, no slippage	4. Clean hydraulic oil, no air bubbles
5. No debris obstructing moving parts	5. Correct coupling
6. Voltage and current within rated values	6. Pump and motor axes properly centered
7. Lever motion within limit values	7. No noise, overheating, or vibration in pump
8. No liquid or vapor on switch	8. No noise, overheating, or vibration in motor

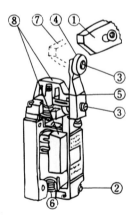
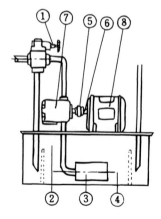

Breakdown Analysis Sheet

Issued by	Group Y, Team 1	What happened		Code no. A 30	section leader	team leader	
Line	Inner 3						
Equipment	GAZI						
Abnormal part	Rubber hose	rubber hose damaged					
time of occurrence	1/23, 9:30 p.m.	repair time	25 minutes	type of	unexpected,		
time restored	1/ 23, 9:55 p.m.	shutdown time	25 minutes	malfunction	recurring		

①

Results of inspection	damage ... table ... machine body ... oil pressure apparatus	Check items Pressure used Bending Twisting Contact with other parts	Inspection results 15 kg/m² (for a 50 k hose) OK none Unclear due to hose damage, but there are traces of contact with the panel

Treatment of problem	1. Replace rubber hose, replenish hydraulic oil 2. Fix hose with supports so it doesn't come into contact with the panel	Code no. B 25. B 31

②

Causes	Parts	Wear caused by contact with the panel and by rubbing	Code no. C 18
	Human actions	We didn't realize that the hose rubbing against other things was an abnormality that could cause a breakdown.	Code no. C 18

③

Preventing recurrence	1. Create a one-point lesson and teach about the abnormality 2. Inspect all equipment for this point	Code no. E 3, E 9

					Date	Person responsible
Team comments We've been overlooking a lot of abnormalities; we have to watch our equipment more carefully.	One - point lesson	needed not needed	Contact with rubber hose		1/28	JY
Section manager's comments The breakdown was handled well. I'd like the team to study the proper state of the equipment further.	Add to autonomous maintenance standards checklist	needed not needed				
	Horizontal deployment	needed not needed	Spot checks of 38 machines in the group		1/26	Team leader

Follow Up on Causes Systematically

Unless we pin down the true causes of a breakdown, we won't be able to prevent the breakdown from happening again. Here are some points to remember when tracking down causes:

1. Develop checklists for the conditions necessary for perfect operation.

2. Check every item on the list for abnormal conditions.

3. Look for human errors that might have contributed to abnormalities.

Analyze and Improve Equipment Inspection Methods

To keep breakdowns from happening again for the same reasons, we need to adjust our own inspection activities.

Critique Current Inspection Methods

1. *Learning to recognize abnormal conditions*

   We need to think critically about why abnormal conditions that led to a breakdown were not discovered ahead of time. Most breakdowns occur because the operators didn't recognize underlying abnormalities as problems. It is important to use actual breakdowns as teaching materials, raising our abilities to spot potential breakdowns on our own.

2. *Performing daily spot checks*

   We may be following the standards in the daily inspection manual for parts affected by debris, wear, or deterioration, but we still have to think critically about certain questions. Do the inspection standards cover all the abnormal conditions that could cause breakdowns? Are the inspection standards correct? If so, why do we still have problems? It's important to take a second look at the inspection standards and continuously update them as breakdown analysis reveals new items to manage.

Improve Inspection Methods

When operators carry out routine daily checks, they tend to assume that they can't prevent breakdowns caused by the deterioration of internal parts, and they don't even try.

Even if we can't observe internal abnormalities while the machine is running, we can at least use our senses to check for external trouble signs like heat, odor, noise, or vibration. If we don't pay attention, we won't be able to predict the service life of our equipment. By staying aware as we watch for abnormalities, we'll be able to predict and deal with them before they cause breakdowns.

Examples of Breakdown Analysis

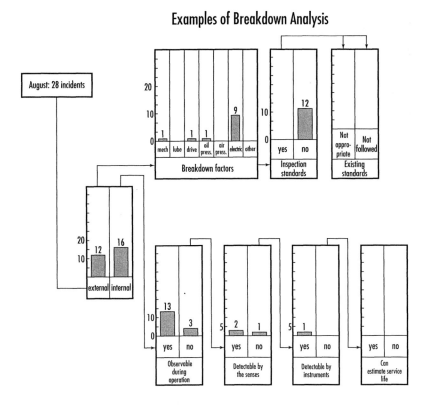

Breakdown Analysis Example—Limit Switch

Team member: The limit switch died, so I replaced it with a new one. They seem to go bad every two years or so, so two years must be their service life.

Maintenance technician: This switch goes on and off once a minute, so according to my calculations, it operates 500,000 times in two years. But the manufacturer says it should be good for 5 million operations, so we're only getting 10 percent of the expected life. What part of it broke?

Team member: I don't know . . . I thought it had outlived its useful life, so I just threw it away.

Maintenance technician: You know, it's not possible to reduce breakdowns without taking a close look at the actual objects that have failed. Next time, let's try to determine which parts broke down.

The team member realized that the maintenance technician had a point, so he got together with other team members and made a thorough study of limit switches. They developed an inspection chart of everything to look at when a switch breaks down. The next time the limit switch broke, they studied the parts, referring to the chart.

34

Inspection Checklist—Limit Switch Breakdown

Check Items	Inspection Results		Check Items	Inspection Results	
1. Correct stop position	*Position normal*	OK	5. No debris on moving parts	*None*	OK
2. Correct limit switch position	*Position normal*	OK	6. Voltage and current within rated values	Rated: AC 200 V 2A Actual: *198 V 1.2A*	OK
3. No play in pin	*No play*	OK	7. Lever motion within limit values	Standard: within 90° Actual: within 60°	OK
4. Roller on track, no slippage	*On track*	OK	8. No liquid or vapor on switch	*Some coolant on switch, but it's waterproof*	✔

Team member: You know, I think it's the service life after all. We checked out the switch according to the chart, and there was nothing wrong.

Maintenance technician: I notice you have a check mark by the item about liquid or vapor on the switch. What's that all about?

Team member: Well, there was some grinding fluid on it, but since this is a waterproof switch, I didn't think it was any big deal.

Maintenance technician: Let's take it apart and look at it.

When they took the switch apart, they discovered that the breakdown was due to an insulation defect caused by grinding fluid and debris inside the switch.

Maintenance technician: Even if a component is "waterproof," vapor and fluid can seep in over time if there are moving parts. It's always best to investigate all possibilities. You can't reach a conclusion without taking the switch apart. The problem was that you didn't recognize that grinding fluid on the switch was a potential cause of the breakdown, right?

Team member: You're right—we have to think beyond our assumptions! I'll teach my teammates about it in a one-point lesson, and we'll check the other equipment for similar problems.

Breakdown Analysis Example—Oil Pressure Pump

This breakdown was a decrease in table drive speed due to insufficient discharge from the oil pressure pump. The team had learned a lot from the breakdown of the limit switch, so they not only checked the actual pump according to the breakdown checklist, but also took the pump apart and inspected the strainer inside it.

Inspection Checklist—Malfunctioning Oil Pressure Pump

Check Items	Inspection Results		Check Items	Inspection Results	
1. Discharge pressure set correctly?	standard: 20±2 kg/cm² actual: 20.5 kg/cm²	OK	5. Coupling normal?	Yes	OK
2. Normal amount of oil in tank?	within level range	OK	6. Pump and motor axes centered?	standard ≤ 1mm off center actual: .08 mm off center	OK
3. Strainer free of debris?	very clogged	✔	7. Noise, overheating, or vibration in pump?	a lot of noise, overheating, and vibration	✔
4. Hydraulic oil clean, no air bubbles?	very dirty, also cloudy	✔	8. Noise, overheating, or vibration in motor?	No	OK

Team leader: When we took the pump apart, we found that the internal parts were extremely worn and the strainer was clogged.

Process engineer: You're talking about wear due to cavitation, right?

Team leader: That's right. We're supposed to check the strainer every three months, but actually, we didn't do it.

Process engineer: Why not? How long does it take?

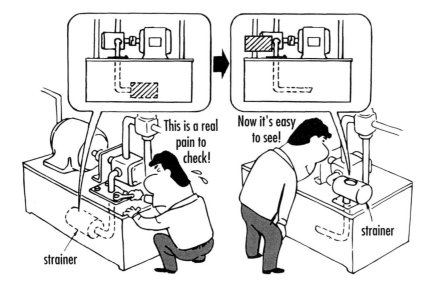

Team leader: Well, the strainer in this machine is really hard to take out, so inspecting it takes about 30 minutes.

Process engineer: So it's not that you just didn't check it; it's more like you *couldn't* check it. You can write all the instructions you want in the inspection standards checklist, but if a procedure takes half an hour, it just won't get done.

Team leader: We're going to find a way to make the strainer easier to inspect.

Process engineer: One more thing. If the internal parts were this worn, they should have been overheating and making a lot of noise. What were you doing to check that?

Team leader: We have noticed that the machine was running noisily, but it's been like that for a long time. There's really nothing in the inspection checklist about noise and overheating.

Process engineer: Okay—I'd better take another look at the inspection standards and add these other items to the checklist right away.

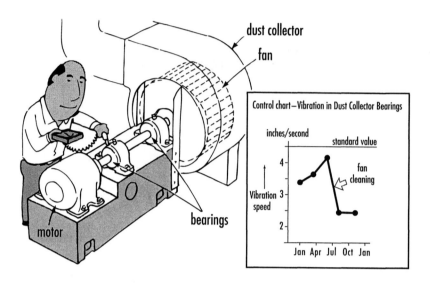

Breakdown Analysis Example—Dust Collector

Team member: The bearings on the dust collector are supposed to be replaced on a three-year cycle, but this time they broke down after two years, and it took seven days to restore them.

Section manager: I wonder why they broke down so soon. Did anything unusual happen?

Team member: We inspected them according to the checklist, but we couldn't find any problems at all. Still, dust was adhering to one side of the fan. That imbalance was the cause of the breakdown, I guess.

Section manager: Does this mean that you need to clean the fan more frequently?

Team member: That cover is way too heavy to take off for a daily check. Wait—I know! The bearings are outside the cover, so we may be able to figure out when the fan is getting imbalanced by measuring their vibration. I'll make that part of the routine right away.

CHAPTER SUMMARY

Many breakdowns result from the cumulative effects of several abnormalities. For this reason, dealing with breakdowns takes more than fixing problems one by one as we notice them. Unless we deal with *all* the abnormalities at once and restore the equipment to its proper state, we won't obtain the results we want. Some problems are unavoidable, but most breakdowns relate to things people can prevent: contamination, running out of lubricant, loose nuts or bolts, neglect of worn parts, or mistakes in operation, changeover, retooling, or repairs.

Eliminating breakdowns requires the help of everyone in the plant. Operators have a special role because we are most familiar with the equipment we use every day.

In TPM, operators clean their machines and check for loose parts. During operation, we watch for abnormal temperature, vibration, sound, and action; keep the lubrication supply at proper levels; and run or retool the equipment according to procedures. This is what we call autonomous maintenance.

The operator's routine daily maintenance activities are a critical first step in eliminating breakdowns, but by themselves they aren't enough. TPM teams need to analyze the breakdowns that occur from day to day, pin down the exact cause of each one, and determine how to adjust routine maintenance activities so causes are detected and treated early.

39

Operators need to understand how their equipment works before they can understand equipment abnormalities. Demonstrating with actual objects and teaching one-point lessons are two approaches to help everyone understand equipment systems and trouble points.

TPM teams should learn the basics about all their equipment subsystems, e.g., fastener, electrical, hydraulic, pneumatic, and drive systems. In that way they can recognize and actively prevent more problems.

Unless we pin down the true causes of a breakdown, we won't be able to prevent the breakdown from happening again. Some tips:

1. Develop checklists for the conditions necessary for perfect operation.

2. Check every item on the list for abnormal conditions.

3. Look for human errors that might have contributed to abnormalities.

We need to critique our current inspection methods and then improve them to make sure they cover the points that allow us to spot problems early. It's important to pay attention and use our senses to catch external trouble signs like heat, odor, noise, or vibration.

Accepting the Challenge of One-Step Defect-Free Changeover

CHAPTER 3

CHAPTER OVERVIEW

Accepting the Challenge of One-Step Defect-Free Changeover

- What Is One-Step Defect-Free Changeover?

- Aiming for One-Step Defect-Free Changeover

- Why We Can't Achieve One-Step Defect-Free Changeover

- Steps for Promoting One-Step Defect-Free Changeover

- Precision Checks for Equipment and Replaceable Parts

- Improve Positioning Methods

- Review Standard Values and Inspection Items to Ensure Equipment Precision

- Take a Second Look at the Machining Conditions

- Draw Up Changeover Standards

- Maintenance and Management

- Summary

What Is One-Step Defect-Free Changeover?

One-step defect-free changeover refers to an approach for setting up the machine for the next product in such a way that the machine produces high-quality goods, starting with the very first item.

In most cases, however, we perform test runs after a changeover, measuring the precision of the processed goods. Then, after we've made the adjustments for each part, we perform even more test runs, repeating the process over and over until we achieve the goal of product precision.

When we adjust the process so many times, we often lose track of our initial positioning. At times, we end up completely redoing the changeover itself.

In contrast, one-step defect-free changeover means changeover with zero adjustments. When we can eliminate adjustments, we can produce 100 percent high-quality goods immediately.

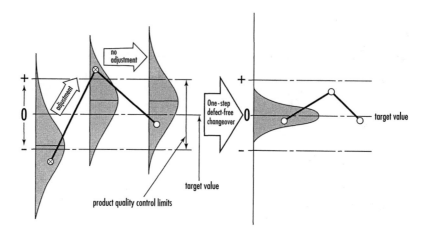

Aiming for One-Step Defect-Free Changeover

Since we don't practice one-step defect-free changeover, we make a lot of readjustments and produce a lot of rejects during the test runs, leading to a lot of wasteful trial and error.

The measured values of the first items produced in the test runs after changeover naturally vary and differ from the target value. If we shift the standard for that reason, the products produced in the continuing processes after this will not necessarily fall within the control limits.

For that reason, it is necessary to have as little variation as possible from the target value at the time of changeover and to set the target and control limits correctly in the first place.

In this way, the target values for one-step defect-free changeover not only prevent defects during the test runs, but more importantly, they prevent defects in the continuous processes afterwards. This means that there's no need for readjustment.

Why We Can't Achieve One-Step Defect-Free Changeover

45

Why can't we achieve one-step defect-free changeover? Here are some common reasons:

1. We assume that adjustments are simply inevitable in a high-precision process.

2. Our equipment and replaceable parts have poor precision, so we make adjustments to compensate.

3. The standard mounting points are not clearly defined with numerical values, so people have to guess at the settings.

4. We don't know the proper machining conditions, or if we do, we aren't applying that knowledge during setup. Furthermore, standard procedures and methods for changeover have not been determined.

If we don't deal with these problems, we can't achieve one-step defect-free changeover.

Steps for Promoting One-Step Defect-Free Changeover

The basic procedure for achieving one-step defect-free change-over is outlined in the flowchart on page 47.

We can start by getting a clear picture of what we're doing during this changeover (see step 1 in the flowchart). We ought to be able to detect a lot of waste just by observing our own procedures carefully. In addition, we'll probably notice how much of our retooling process is devoted to test runs and adjustments.

To eliminate adjustments, let's start with the simple things. First of all, let's make sure that we've checked the precision of the equipment and replaceable parts and done all we can to improve the positioning (see steps 3 and 4). We'll be able to eliminate a lot of the need for adjustments just with these steps.

When it comes to the more difficult adjustments that remain (see steps 6–10), use the more rigorous P-M analysis methods described in Chapter 1.

Finally, maintain and manage the new standard by following autonomous maintenance standards to reduce variability in equipment conditions, tracking changeover conditions, and monitoring tool precision on an ongoing basis.

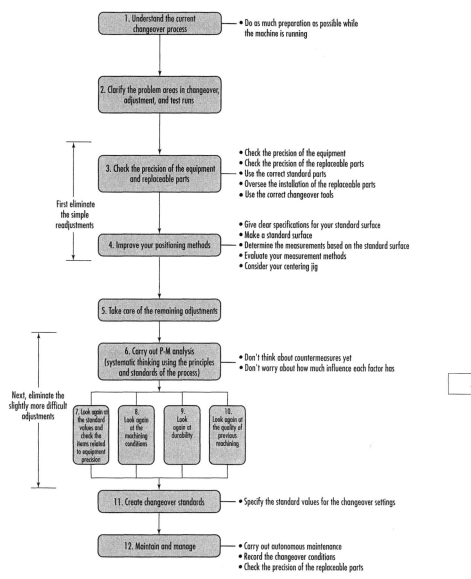

Precision Checks for Equipment and Replaceable Parts

If you visit a plant that can't produce the correct dimensions without making adjustments, you're likely to find dirty equipment that is never cleaned and machines with excessive vibration and play in the components. Furthermore, if you look at the replaceable parts, you'll find that their surfaces are unusually worn and that the operators don't seem to mind using parts that are scratched or rusty.

Some workplaces don't even have replaceable tools, so they make do with regrinding the old tools to fit. Does this sound like your workplace?

If this is what our workplace is like, no amount of improvement in our procedures will let us achieve one-step defect-free changeover.

We have to begin by checking the precision of our equipment and fixing anything that's not working right. At the same time, we need to *check the precision of the replaceable parts* and be sure to *manage in sets* the ones whose norms are correct.

At times, we also find cases in which operators are not using the correct changeover tools. Instead of thinking that one tool is as good as another, remember that this too can affect precision and the need for adjustments.

There's no way we'll get one-step zero defects in a place like this!

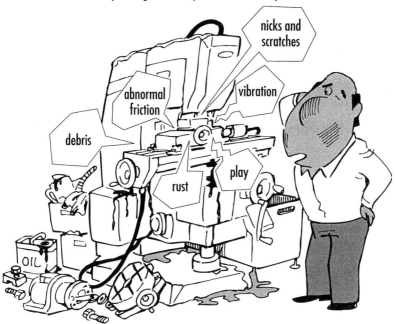

49

Improve Positioning Methods

Maybe you find yourself always having to adjust the centering and proportions of the workpiece.

In most cases, this happens because we haven't defined standard mounting points well enough, so that should be our first step.

Another common problem, even if we have standard mounting points, is that the positioning measurements are not clearly defined in relation to the mounting points. In such cases, we have to study the dimensions of the workpiece and the replaceable parts and determine the measurements from the standard mounting points.

The example pictured on the opposite page shows what happened in a plant where they used to adjust the strokes each time the dimensions of the workpiece changed. When the central processing position of the workpiece was made uniform, the strokes also became uniform, eliminating the need for adjustments.

Once we have decided on the positioning measurements in relation to the standard mounting points, we should next set them firmly. To accomplish this, we may want to use positioning blocks, attach a scale plate (a plate with a graduated scale for settings) or a dial gauge, or attach a centering jig or other such tools to allow one-touch setting.

If we follow the procedures described above, most of our adjustments will be eliminated, and we can achieve one-step defect-free changeover. Challenge yourself to see if you can achieve one-step defect-free changeover in your plant.

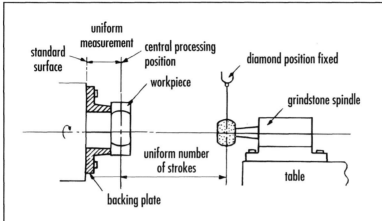

Take another look at the thickness of the backing plate to make sure that
the measurements from the standard surface to the center
processing position are uniform.

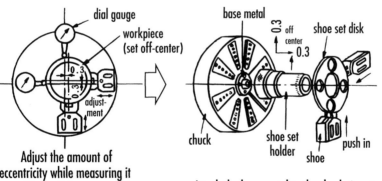

Adjust the amount of
eccentricity while measuring it
with the dial gauge to
determine the shoe position.

Attach the base metal to the chuck, insert
the already off-center shoe set holder, then
join it with the shoe set disk and set it
with a single motion by pushing in the shoe.

Review Standard Values and Inspection Items to Ensure Equipment Precision

How can we eliminate the more difficult adjustments that remain after we've implemented the improvements described in the previous pages? The first step is to think about the reasons for the adjustments in the light of the principles and standards of the process. We need to make a thorough review of the standard values, the inspection items, the precision of our equipment, the machining conditions, the rigidity of the tool and workpiece, and the quality of any previous machining.

The following example illustrates the process of reviewing the precision of the equipment and the machining conditions.

Typically, when we change the cutting tool on an NC lathe, the machining measurements vary with each changeover, even with the tool firmly secured in the holder, so after the test cuts, we measure the dimensions of the machined workpiece and make tool corrections.

Applying P-M analysis as soon as we detect varying dimensions leads us to reevaluate the precision of the equipment. As a result, we find that only 20 percent of the tool holder's surface contacts the tool. Furthermore, the tightness of the bolt varies, so the tip of the tool shifts as much as 0.09 mm.

We regrind the tool contact surface on the holder and correct the contact to 70 percent. After hand-tightening both bolts, we use a torque wrench to secure them with a standard force. As a result, the tip of the cutting tool is held steady, and we achieve one-step defect-free changeover.

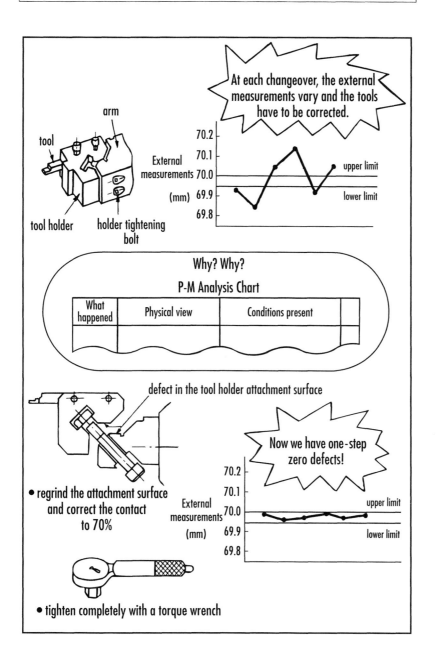

arm

tool

External
measurements (mm)

70.2
70.1
70.0
69.9
69.8

At each changeover, the external
measurements vary and the tools
have to be corrected.

upper limit

lower limit

tool holder

holder tightening
bolt

Why? Why?

P-M Analysis Chart

What happened	Physical view	Conditions present	

defect in the tool holder attachment surface

- regrind the attachment surface
  and correct the contact
  to 70%

External
measurements (mm)

70.2
70.1
70.0
69.9
69.8

Now we have one-step
zero defects!

upper limit

lower limit

- tighten completely with a torque wrench

Take a Second Look at the Machining Conditions

You'd be surprised to learn how often operators have to make repeated adjustments simply because the machining conditions have been set up poorly. In some of these cases, the machining conditions themselves are vague or haven't been determined at all.

The next example concerns an outer diameter grinding process in which the concentricity was off, despite the fact that there was no problem with the precision of either the equipment or the replaceable parts. Because of this problem, the operators had to divide the process into rough grinding and finish grinding, making a lot of adjustments along the way.

Here's what they found when they took a second look at the principles of the process:

1. There was a difference between the ideal and actual angles of the shoes that supported the workpiece.

2. There was a difference between the ideal and actual offset (the amount that the center of the workpiece is off from the center of revolution).

When they reset the angles of the front and rear shoes and the workpiece offset to their ideal values, the concentricity defects that had caused so many headaches completely disappeared and the operators no longer had to split the processes or make adjustments.

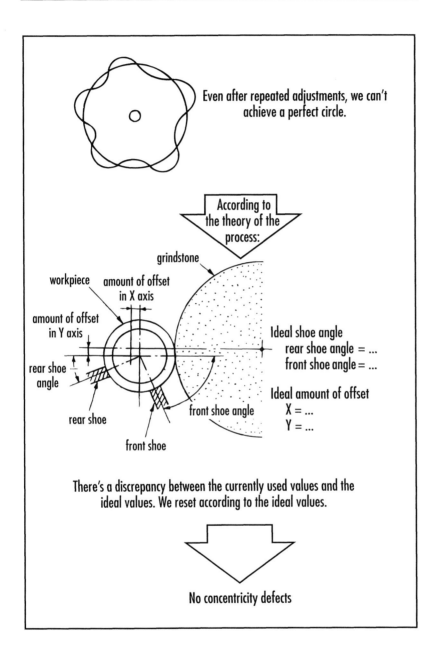

Even after repeated adjustments, we can't achieve a perfect circle.

According to the theory of the process:

grindstone

workpiece   amount of offset in X axis

amount of offset in Y axis

rear shoe angle

rear shoe

front shoe angle

front shoe

Ideal shoe angle
rear shoe angle = ...
front shoe angle = ...

Ideal amount of offset
X = ...
Y = ...

There's a discrepancy between the currently used values and the ideal values. We reset according to the ideal values.

No concentricity defects

55

Draw Up Changeover Standards

In many cases workplaces have achieved one-step defect-free changeover, only to drift back into old patterns with the passage of time or with a turnover in personnel. To keep this from happening, we need to draw up changeover standards, standardizing the conditions and procedures for retooling so that anyone can implement them.

If we do this, we can look at a situation in which the one-step defect-free changeover system has fallen apart and see which of the changeover conditions deviates from the standards. With this understanding, we can more easily work out solutions. Like the standards for autonomous maintenance, the standards for one-step defect-free changeover should be clearly defined and rigorously maintained.

We can't be content with just drawing up changeover standards. We should organize our procedures so that we have a record of the changeover conditions at each retooling. Only then can we truly claim to follow changeover standards.

An example of a log page for recording changeover conditions appears on the opposite page.

Changeover Conditions Log				Standard number		Change-over	Date
							Operator
Process	Outer ring raceway grinding Inner circumference	Machine model	72 Improved	Malfunctions (quality breakdown)			
Standards to be recorded	Items		Mark a circle next to items corrected				
	Work cycle speed						
	Grindstone cycle speed (grindstone large—small)						
	Plunge speed						
	Plate edge surface vibrating						
	Plate and shoe contact						

Items	Measurement method	Degree of precision		
		Standard	Before correction	After correction
Changeover conditions				
Backing plate edge surface shaking	$\dfrac{1}{100}$ (dial gauge)	±0		
Align the product and work axes exactly	magnet ON $\dfrac{1}{100}$ (dial gauge)	vibration 0.005		
Positioning the shoe	$\dfrac{1}{100}$ (dial gauge)	A= 0.15 B= 0.15		

57

Maintenance and Management

So what is the most important thing to keep in mind for maintaining and managing one-step defect-free changeover? Of course, we should create changeover standards and record the changeover conditions. However, it is also extremely important to make a habit of autonomous maintenance. To prevent the loss of precision in our equipment and replacement parts, we must also follow our own cleaning and inspection standards strictly. A workplace that doesn't practice autonomous maintenance can't achieve one-step defect-free changeover.

Furthermore, it is important to keep good track of the parts and measuring tools that we know to be precise. We need to come up with ways of handling and storing them that will keep them clean and prevent the formation of nicks, dents, wear, or rust.

CHAPTER SUMMARY

In most changeovers, we perform test runs to check the precision of the processed goods. After adjustments, we do more test runs, repeating the process over and over until we achieve product precision. After so many adjustments, we often lose track of our initial positioning. At times, we end up completely redoing the changeover itself.

In contrast, one-step defect-free changeover means changeover with zero adjustments. When we can eliminate adjustments, we can produce 100 percent high-quality goods immediately.

Our changeovers involve repeated adjustments for several reasons:

1. We assume that adjustments are simply inevitable in a high-precision process.

2. Our equipment and replaceable parts have poor precision, so we make adjustments to compensate.

3. The standard mounting points are not clearly defined with numerical values, so people have to guess at the settings.

4. We don't know the proper machining conditions, or if we do, we don't apply that knowledge during setup. Furthermore, standard procedures and methods for changeover have not been determined.

The procedure for achieving one-step defect-free changeover begins with understanding what we're doing during changeover. It involves checking the precision of equipment and replaceable parts, and improving positioning methods so the position can be set to standard, repeatable numeric values. Finally, we establish changeover standards, and then maintain and manage them by following autonomous maintenance standards to reduce variability in equipment conditions, tracking changes in conditions, and monitoring tool precision on an ongoing basis.

Dealing with
Minor Stoppages

CHAPTER 4

CHAPTER OVERVIEW

Dealing with Minor Stoppages

- Minor Stoppages Wipe Out the Advantages of Automation

- How Minor Stoppages Lead to Major Losses

- Why Minor Stoppages Are Not Taken Seriously

- Approaches for Eliminating Minor Stoppages

- Gain a Clear Idea of Losses

- Deal with Slight Abnormalities

- Analyze the Situation

- Investigate Causes and Deal with Problem Areas

- Determine Optimal Conditions

- Examples of Measures against Minor Stoppages

- Advice for TPM Teams

- Summary

Disruptions of unattended operations lasting 60 minutes or more
(combined total for 15 grinding lines)

Minor Stoppages Wipe out the Advantages of Automation

Minor stoppages are different from normal breakdowns: They're situations when the equipment either shuts down or idles due to a temporary problem. This problem particularly affects automated processes that could otherwise run unattended.

In a plant with multiple machines, a minor stoppage shuts down production for only a little while, assuming it's discovered in time. If it goes unnoticed for a long time, however, it may lead to long delays as work gets backed up at earlier processes. Just one minor stoppage can wipe out the advantages of automation.

The pie charts show the downtime recorded in one plant that was trying to automate. As you can see, nearly one-third of all disruptions were due to minor stoppages, mostly in delivery and supply mechanisms.

63

How Minor Stoppages Lead to Major Losses

A look at the effects of minor stoppages shows the negative influence they have on many aspects of production.

1. *The overall effectiveness of the equipment drops.* Minor stoppages and delays in correcting them reduce the performance rate of the equipment. This directly affects its *overall equipment effectiveness* (OEE), a commonly used TPM metric.

2. *Other linked machines are idled.* In a plant where operators attend multiple linked machines, minor stoppages keep people busy, distracting them from their usual work with the other machines. As the other machines finish their cycles and pause, the whole cell is delayed while the stoppage is corrected.

3. *Product quality defects increase.* When workpieces get stuck or are otherwise held up during minor stoppages, they tend to become worn or deformed, and this eventually leads to quality defects.

4. *Idle machines mean energy losses.* Shutting down or idling machines wastes electricity and fuel.

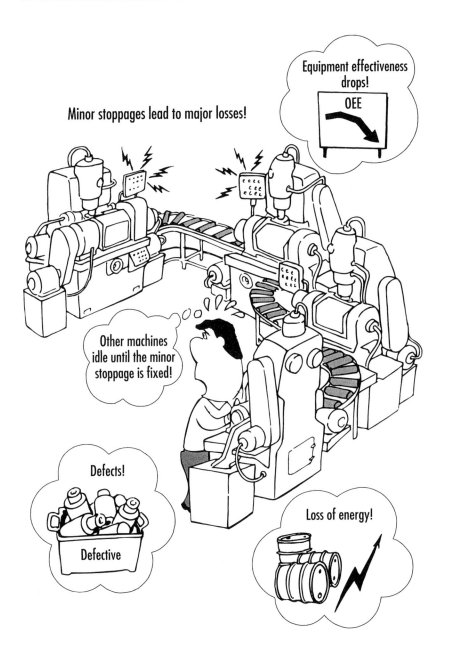

Why Minor Stoppages Are Not Taken Seriously

Let's consider the reasons why companies often don't take minor stoppages seriously, even though they can lead to huge losses.

1. *The size of the loss isn't obvious.* Depending on how frequently they occur, minor stoppages may not look like obvious losses. We often don't take them seriously because they seem small—we're unaware of how much loss they can cause.

2. *We treat the symptoms.* Since our investigations of minor stoppages are superficial, we end up making emergency, on-the-spot adjustments, or we try to get by with half-baked, partial measures. In other words, we try to treat the symptoms instead of the disease.

3. *We don't do enough on-site inspection or observation.* Even if we try to make accurate on-site observations, we may not happen to witness any minor stoppages. When we do encounter them, they often happen so fast that we can't get a clear picture of what occurred.

Approaches for Eliminating Minor Stoppages

Now let's look at some steps and hints for dealing with minor stoppages and bringing them down to zero.

Steps	Hints
1. Get a clear idea of the loss.	Take a closer look at the losses from minor stoppages. See if you can express them numerically.
2. Take care of slight abnormalities.	Slight abnormalities in the product or the processing equipment (ones that may or may not cause trouble) should be looked at one by one and treated as real problems.
3. Analyze the current situation.	Observe the situation carefully and analyze it. Consider every condition you find, without worrying about how likely it is to cause trouble.
4. Investigate every factor; identify and treat all abnormal conditions.	Don't be bound by previous criteria for judging what's important. Analyze not only the malfunctions but also everything that might be a symptom of a malfunction.
5. Determine optimal conditions.	Don't assume that machine or conveyor parts and units are currently attached and assembled in the most appropriate ways.

The next sections deal with each of these steps in more detail.

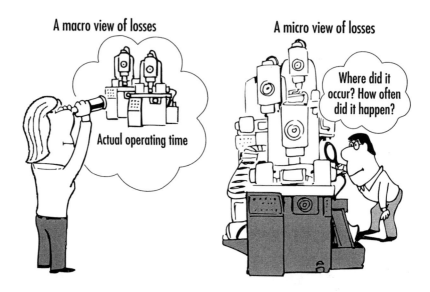

A macro view of losses

A micro view of losses

Actual operating time

Where did it occur? How often did it happen?

Gain a Clear Idea of Losses

Losses from minor stoppages are a huge problem precisely because we don't notice how large they are cumulatively. To eliminate minor stoppages, we absolutely must recognize them as losses.

There are two methods for getting a picture of losses: the macro method and the micro method. The macro method involves determining the equipment's actual operating time, then seeing whether it has achieved an appropriate level of productivity. This helps us calculate the extent of losses due to minor stoppages.

The micro method involves looking at the components and parts where minor stoppages have occurred and noting how often they occur.

Deal with Slight Abnormalities

One approach for dealing with slight abnormalities is to clean the equipment thoroughly. This is especially important for parts where the workpiece moves or passes through. Remember that cleaning means inspection; as we clean, we can discover signs of abnormalities, even if they haven't caused any malfunctions yet. Cleaning is an opportunity to monitor such tiny flaws and learn how much they might be contributing to minor stoppages.

To reduce minor stoppages, we must painstakingly identify potential symptoms of malfunctions in areas that may or may not be malfunctioning. Then we need to correct these symptoms.

Even if fixing minor flaws doesn't eliminate all minor stoppages, it teaches us to pay attention to parts that aren't quite in their normal state, which will lead us to solutions more easily.

71

Be sure you have an accurate understanding of any minor stoppages.

Analyze the Situation

72

Confirm What Happened

If we're going to eliminate minor stoppages, we must observe them closely and analyze them carefully.

Since most people don't take minor stoppage losses seriously, it's safe to say that we rarely understand how they happen. So we should first classify minor stoppages according to the forms in which they appear and then study their frequencies and locations.

To gain a clear idea of the actual situations, we may need to use video cameras, high-speed still cameras, or even high-speed video cameras to capture what actually happens in a stoppage.

Analyze What Happened

Analyzing the situation requires us to sort out the levels of detail correctly and look at the problem from a physical point of view. In every situation, that's a matter of tracing the physical principles that govern the process. For example, when workpieces are backed up in a supply chute, we can determine that it's due to high friction resistance.

Next, we need to get a clear picture of the circumstances in which the situation arises. When we find that certain conditions always give rise to similar problems, we can classify them accordingly.

For example, we might group together cases caused by excess friction resistance between the workpieces and the chute, or by the workpieces' getting jumbled together. After that, we can break down the causes further, looking at the relationships among the equipment, tools, and workpieces. Then we list every possible cause we find at every possible level.

Investigate Causes and Deal with Problem Areas

74

As we identify all abnormalities that are causing trouble, it's important not to get caught up in old ways of looking at things or to be bound by previously accepted criteria for what matters and what doesn't. Instead, we have to look at how the process was originally meant to work. When we can't tell whether something is normal or abnormal, it's better to add it to the list, just to be sure.

Often it's those borderline cases that are most likely to cause trouble. If we don't know how something is supposed to function, we need to think through its workings, determine its optimal state, and then look for abnormalities by comparing the actual state to the optimal state.

It's very important to thoroughly deal with and devise countermeasures for all the malfunctions that we pick out.

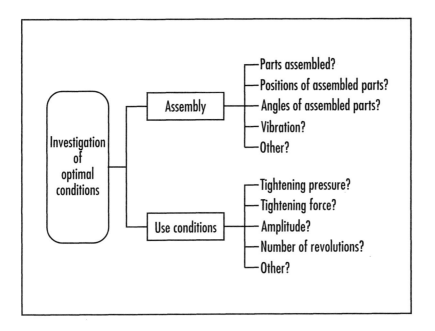

Determine Optimal Conditions

Determining optimal conditions involves asking whether the equipment parts and units are assembled in the most appropriate ways and whether they are used in the most appropriate manner. The conditions we observe are usually based on people's past experience and on extensions of past technology.

Usually these current conditions are not optimal. We need to study the assembly and use of the equipment to discover the best approach. The diagram shows an example of some points to consider related to machining equipment.

75

Examples of Measures against Minor Stoppages

To see how we might take measures against minor stoppages, let's look at a case in which an automatic bearing assembler keeps stopping because the supply of steel balls is interrupted.

First, we determine the extent of the minor stoppage. We find that in the course of making 1,000 bearings, the steel ball fails to come through as many as 18 out of 30 times. Then we systematically review the reasons why this is happening.

When we look at the actual equipment, we discover a lot of abnormal conditions. After restoring the proper conditions point by point, we find that the steel balls now fail to come out only 1.3 times per thousand bearings, or only 1/15 of the frequency before improvement.

1. Think Systematically about Minor Stoppages

What happened	Physical view	Conditions	Relation of equipment and the tools		Inspection results
Not enough balls	The designated number of balls does not roll into the shutter within a given period of time.	The balls get stuck on the way because of friction resistance between the balls and the surfaces they contact.	The balls get jammed against each other in gaps in the sleeve.	• Hopper cylinder is off center • Large gaps in the sleeve • Many joints in the sleeve	✔ ✔ —
			The balls bridge the opening in the receiver hopper.	• Relation of the ball hopper shape and the ball measurements	—

2. Improve All the Problem Areas You Find

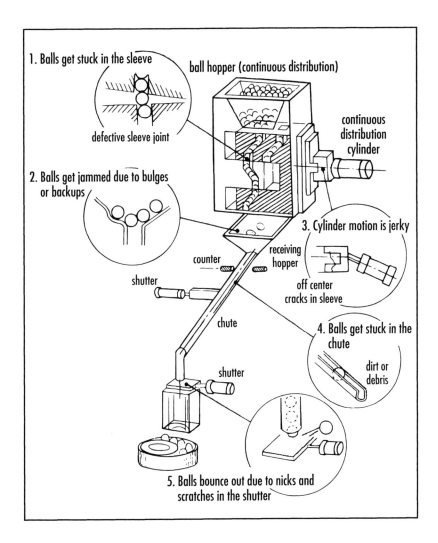

1. Balls get stuck in the sleeve

defective sleeve joint

ball hopper (continuous distribution)

continuous distribution cylinder

2. Balls get jammed due to bulges or backups

counter

shutter

receiving hopper

3. Cylinder motion is jerky

off center cracks in sleeve

chute

shutter

4. Balls get stuck in the chute

dirt or debris

5. Balls bounce out due to nicks and scratches in the shutter

77

3. Confirm the Results

Advice for TPM Teams

Throughout this chapter, we have been discussing ways to combat minor stoppages.

When a TPM team begins working on equipment loss improvements, they often study the six big equipment-related losses and then start with the problems that look easiest to resolve. Often, however, the fix that looks easy at first glance turns out to be more complicated when we get into it. We have to throw out old assumptions and adopt new methods that work.

In the future, zero minor stoppages will be an essential goal in every workplace that is aiming for partial and full automation. Following the approaches we have discussed here should make it less difficult to eliminate waste and loss from minor stoppages.

CHAPTER SUMMARY

Minor stoppages are different from normal breakdowns: They're situations when the equipment either shuts down or idles due to a temporary problem. This problem particularly affects automated processes that could otherwise run unattended.

In a plant with multiple machines, a minor stoppage shuts down production for only a little while, assuming it's discovered in time. If it goes unnoticed for a long time, however, it may lead to long delays as work gets backed up at earlier processes. Just one minor stoppage can wipe out the advantages of automation:

1. The overall effectiveness of the equipment drops.

2. Other linked machines are idled.

3. Product quality defects increase.

4. Idle machines mean energy losses.

To eliminate minor stoppages, we must first recognize that these minor-seeming problems have a large cumulative effect. We can do this by measuring the actual operating time or keeping track of how often particular minor stoppages occur.

The next step is to deal with slight abnormalities. Cleaning the equipment is an opportunity to monitor these tiny flaws and learn how much they might be contributing to minor stoppages. Even if fixing minor flaws doesn't eliminate all minor stoppages, it teaches us to pay attention to places that aren't quite in their normal state, which will lead us to solutions more easily.

79

The next step is to analyze the situations when minor stoppages occur. This involves categorizing them and sometimes capturing them using a high-speed video camera. Then we have to look at what is physically happening, grouping problems that arise under similar conditions.

When the physical problem is understood, we investigate causes and deal with problem areas. It's important not to get caught up in old ways of looking at things; rather, we have to look at how the process was originally meant to work. If we don't know how something is supposed to function, we need to think through its workings, determine its optimal state, and then look for abnormalities by comparing the actual state to the optimal state.

Finally, we determine the optimal conditions, including asking whether the equipment parts and units are assembled in the most appropriate ways and whether they are used in the most appropriate manner.

Dealing with
Speed Loss

CHAPTER 5

CHAPTER OVERVIEW

Dealing with Speed Loss

- • What Is Speed Loss?
- • The Reasons for Speed Loss
- • Steps for Dealing with Speed Loss
- • Investigate the Current State and Past Problems
- • How to Find Speed Losses Quickly
- • How to Find Out When Idling and Air Cuts Occur
- • Compare Equipment Specifications with the Current State
- • Pinpoint and Treat Problem Areas
- • Maintain Optimal Conditions
- • Example of an Inspection and Service Standards Chart
- • Summary

82

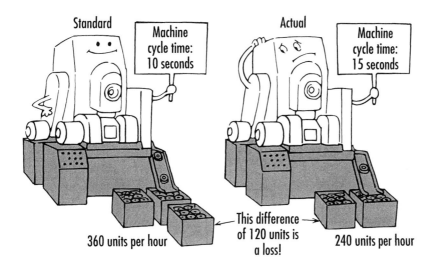

Standard

Machine cycle time: 10 seconds

Actual

Machine cycle time: 15 seconds

360 units per hour

This difference of 120 units is a loss!

240 units per hour

What Is Speed Loss?

Speed loss is an hourly loss that occurs when equipment is run at a lower speed than its standard or rated speed. Some factories think of machine speed and speed loss in terms of parts produced per hour. In TPM we often calculate speed loss by looking at the difference between the standard and the actual machine cycle times of the equipment.

For example, if the standard cycle time is 10 seconds, then it should be possible to machine 6 items per minute, or 360 items per hour. However, if the actual machine cycle time is 15 seconds, then only 64 items can be machined per minute, which is 240 items an hour.

This difference of $360 - 240 = 120$ items per hour is the hourly speed loss. This speed loss is stated as a percentage of the standard rate by using the following formula:

$$\frac{\text{standard machine cycle time (10)}}{\text{actual machine cycle time (15)}} \times 100 = 66\%$$

The Reasons for Speed Loss

It is important to understand the reasons for speed loss before we try to devise countermeasures for it. Here are three of the conceivable reasons:

1. We mistakenly believe that the current machine cycle time is normal.

2. We must slow down the machine cycle to avoid problems.

3. The equipment was poorly designed.

The third factor indicates a problem on the design end, but the first two factors are under the users' control.

Belief that the Current Cycle Time Is Normal

Most often, we assume that the current machine speed is the standard speed. The equipment may operate at its standard machine cycle time initially, but once trouble occurs, we make only a halfhearted attempt to search for the causes. Since the cycle time remains slow, we get used to it and think it's normal.

Slowing Down to Avoid Problems

Often we slow equipment down because running it at its design speed results in lowered product quality and mechanical problems. There can be many causes, including flaws in the static precision of the equipment or the precision of the fixtures and tools.

Steps for Dealing with Speed Loss

The flowchart shows a process for dealing with speed loss. The following sections explore the main steps of this process in more detail.

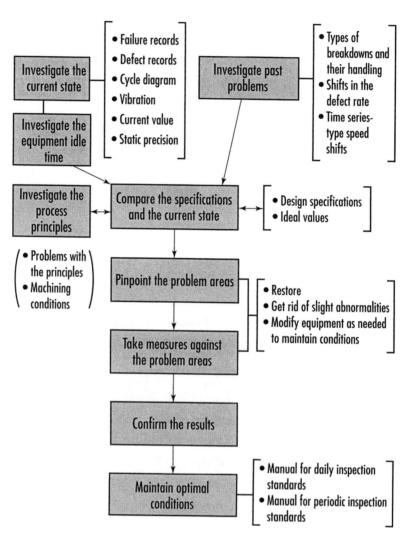

Current situation

Check vibration values, current values, etc.

Past history

Review records of problems such as breakdowns and defect rates

Investigate the Current State and Past Problems

Our basic procedure should be first to understand the current state of the equipment and any past trouble.

To study the current state of our equipment, we look at what kinds of malfunctions and defects occur most often. In addition, we can use a monitoring device to record the processing cycle time, and also observe the vibration and the flow of current during machining.

Besides studying the current state, we investigate past problems by looking at maintenance records. We see what kinds of breakdowns have occurred, how they were dealt with, and what the results were, as well as the defect rate and how it has changed over time.

87

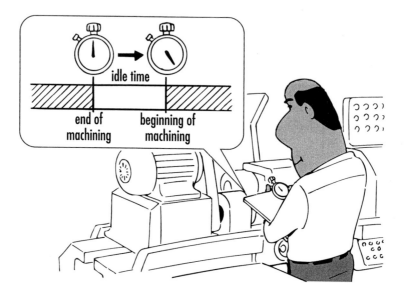

How to Find Speed Losses Quickly

As we investigate the current performance of the equipment, we may get a sense that the machine is idling much of the time. There are two methods we can use to measure how much of each cycle is idle time.

1. Using a stopwatch, we can measure the time that elapses between the end of one cycle and the beginning of the next.

2. We can use a monitoring device to create a graph of the machine cycle and determine the idle time from this data.

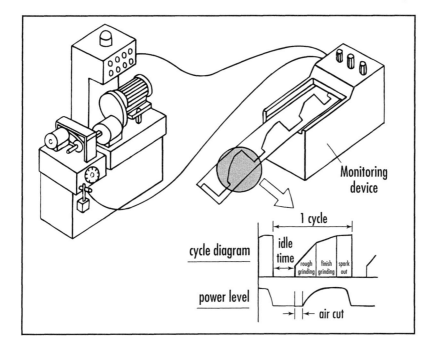

Monitoring device

cycle diagram

power level

1 cycle

idle time

rough grinding | finish grinding | spark out

air cut

How to Find Out When Idling and Air Cuts Occur

With a simple monitoring device, we can create a graph to represent the equipment motion—the rotation of a grinder, for example—during each cycle. The "flat" part of the cycle graph that indicates no motion is the idle time between cycles, such as the time it takes the machine to return to the starting position.

If we also monitor the power applied to move the tool against the workpiece and compare it to the cycle graph, we may find a period at the beginning or end of each cycle when the tool is working but is not cutting anything. This period represents "air cut" time, which extends the machine cycle time unnecessarily.

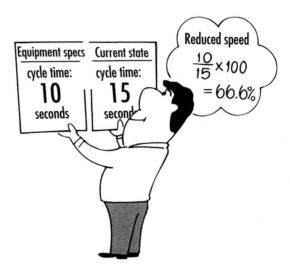

Compare Equipment Specifications with the Current State

We can determine the extent of the speed loss by comparing the equipment specifications and its current state.

When the machine cycle time is indicated in the equipment specifications, we can figure out the speed loss at a glance by comparing that value with the actual machine cycle time and applying the formula given on page 83.

The cycle time is not always spelled out in the machine specifications, however. In such cases, do not seek to establish the standard machine cycle time by taking the number of machining processes required in one day and dividing that by the working time. Rather, follow the logical principles of the process to arrive at a theoretical value and base the standard machine cycle time on that theoretical value.

Pinpoint and Treat Problem Areas

Once we understand the extent of the speed loss, we can finally turn to devising countermeasures.

First, we must clean the equipment. This is important, because we can find malfunctions or symptoms of malfunctions during cleaning. In TPM, we use cleaning as a thorough inspection to help us uncover most of the problem areas.

As we discover problems that could be affecting the machine cycle time, we can restore the equipment, eliminate slight abnormalities, or if necessary modify machine elements to better control processing conditions. The next sections share examples that use these approaches.

An Example of Restoration

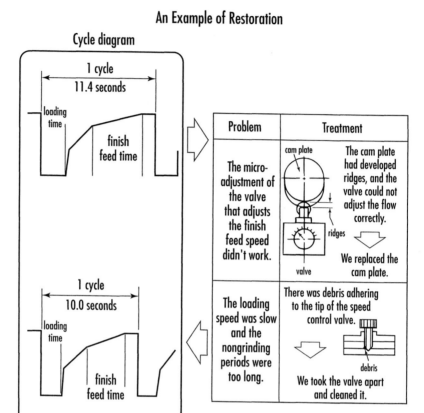

Cycle diagram

Problem	Treatment
The micro-adjustment of the valve that adjusts the finish feed speed didn't work.	The cam plate had developed ridges, and the valve could not adjust the flow correctly. We replaced the cam plate.
The loading speed was slow and the nongrinding periods were too long.	There was debris adhering to the tip of the speed control valve. We took the valve apart and cleaned it.

92

Restore the Equipment

In the example shown here, the equipment's standard machine cycle time was 10 seconds, but the actual machine cycle time was 11.4 seconds. By restoring two trouble spots, the TPM team got the cycle time back to 10.0 seconds, bringing speed loss down to zero.

Develop an eye for slight abnormalities

What do we have here, a little flaw?

Eliminate Slight Abnormalities

When shortening the machine cycle time makes equipment produce low-quality goods, we can usually solve the problem by restoring any abnormal conditions we find. However, sometimes restoration doesn't reduce the machine cycle time as much as we hoped.

Often this is because we've ignored slight abnormalities. When we're operating according to conventional wisdom, these abnormalities appear insignificant, so we tend to overlook them. After all, we think, they are unlikely to have any effect on our results.

Thus, even if we use routine cleaning as an opportunity to discover malfunctions, we overlook tiny flaws because we haven't developed an eye for spotting them.

93

Eliminating Minor Abnormalities

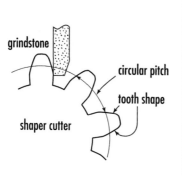

Oil purity	Error in circular pitch when machined at standard speed
Level 12	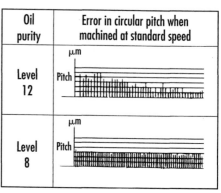
Level 8	

In one example, the operators noticed the presence of minute particles of debris and dirt in the machining oil, but they didn't realize that this tiny flaw might affect the operation.

Nevertheless, when they ground teeth in a gear shaper cutter at the standard machine speed, the precision of the circular pitch deviated from the norm, so the operators ran it more slowly, extending the machine cycle time to 1.6 times the standard.

Then someone recognized that dirt in the hydraulic oil might be a tiny flaw that affected precision at the standard speed. After the operators began strictly controlling the purity of the oil, the degree of purity improved by four levels. As a result, the operators were able to stabilize the precision of the circular pitch while running the machine at the standard speed.

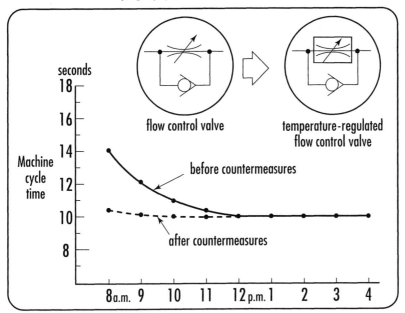

Modifying Equipment to Control Conditions

Modify the Equipment to Control Conditions

Machine operators sometimes run into problems on equipment with a hydraulic drive because the amount of oil passing through the flow control valve fluctuates as the oil's viscosity increases or decreases with temperature changes. The result is often a speed loss from increased machine cycle time after the morning startup, especially in the winter.

To counteract this, we can replace the ordinary flow control valve with one that compensates for temperature and pressure. Simple modifications like this can control conditions to keep the machine cycle time uniform, even after initial startup, and reduce speed loss to zero.

Maintain Optimal Conditions

96

We may make some effort to restore our equipment to its original state or better, but if we stop there, speed loss will occur again. That's why it's extremely important to maintain the equipment in optimal condition.

To do that, we first have to understand the optimal condition in quantifiable terms. This means using drawings and numbers to record the machining conditions, the cycle diagram, vibration during machining, the current flow, static precision, and other factors.

This record becomes a new standard we can use during routine periodic inspection to check for any changes in these conditions. We need to watch continuously for deterioration and prevent it at the source so that we can maintain our equipment in its proper condition and keep it running at the standard speed.

Example of an Inspection and Service Standards Chart

Inspection and Service Standards							
Name of equipment	Outer ring race grinder			Model		GR-5	
No.	Check Items	Evaluation Standards	Inspection Method	Steps Taken	Work Area	Time	Cycle
1	Compensating feed handle shaft	Play in diameter axis, MAX 0.05	1/1,000 test indicator	Change bearings	D	5 min.	6 months
2	Wear on brake plate	Wear depth MAX 0.3	Slide calipers	Polishing compensation	A	3 min.	12 months
3							6 months

CHAPTER SUMMARY

Speed loss is an hourly loss that occurs when equipment is run at a lower speed than its standard or rated speed. In TPM we often calculate speed loss by looking at the difference between the standard and the actual machine cycle times of the equipment.

Speed loss happens for three reasons:

1. We mistakenly believe that the current machine cycle time is normal.

2. We must slow down the machine cycle to avoid problems.

3. The equipment was poorly designed.

TPM teams can address the first two factors through focused improvement. The first step is to investigate the current state of the equipment to understand what kind of malfunctions and defects occur most often. We may also use monitoring devices to record the processing cycle time, observe vibration, and so on. We also check maintenance records for past problems and how they were dealt with.

Idle time often contributes to speed losses. We can determine how much of the cycle is idle time by using a stopwatch or a special monitoring device that graphs the powered motion of the machine. This monitoring helps us see when the machine is taking a long time to return to the starting position or is making "air cuts" (powered but not touching the workpiece).

We can determine the extent of the speed loss by comparing the equipment specifications and its current state. In some cases we may need to determine the standard machine cycle time theoretically, based on process principles.

Once we understand the extent of the speed loss, we can finally turn to devising countermeasures.

First, we must clean the equipment. Cleaning is also a thorough inspection to help us uncover the problem areas. As we discover problems that could affect the machine cycle time, we can restore the equipment, eliminate slight abnormalities, or if necessary modify machine elements to better control processing conditions.

If we stop making these efforts, speed loss will occur again, so it's extremely important to maintain the equipment in optimal condition. To do that, we first have to understand the optimal condition in quantifiable terms, using drawings and numbers to record machining conditions, the cycle diagram, vibration, current flow, static precision, and other factors. This record becomes a new standard for use during routine periodic inspection.

Using Equipment to Build in Quality

CHAPTER 6

CHAPTER OVERVIEW

Using Equipment to Build in Quality

- The Times Demand Quality

- Aim for Zero Defects

- What Is Quality Maintenance?

- Sporadic Defects and Chronic Defects

- Ideas for Reducing Chronic Defects

- Basic Principles of Quality Maintenance

- Setting Things Up So Defects Don't Occur

- Managing Conditions

- Making Inspections Easier

- The First Step: Completely Eliminating Accelerated Deterioration

- From Adjustment to Control

- Summary

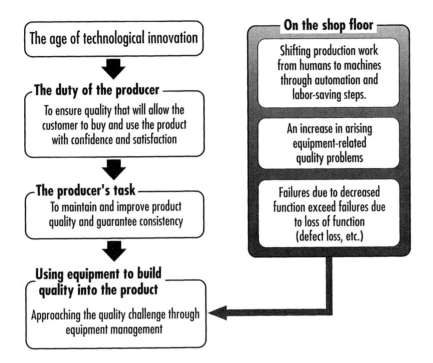

The Times Demand Quality

Reliable product quality is a prerequisite for doing business today. This makes it especially important for us as production workers to maintain and raise the product quality and to ensure uniform quality for our customers.

At the same time, our plants are becoming more sophisticated, automated, and energy efficient, shifting much of the responsibility for quality from people to machines. This motivates us to focus on the condition of our equipment to maintain product quality. This chapter shares some pointers for using the equipment to build quality into the product.

Aim for Zero Defects

Most of the time, we deal with quality defects by analyzing the ones that we see, figuring out the contributing factors, and devising countermeasures, beginning with the major problems. However, this approach is like going after gophers the last place we saw one. We may eliminate them in one place, but they pop up again and we never completely eliminate them.

To achieve zero defects, we can't just take care of the defects as they pop up. Instead, we have to think about how to prevent them from occurring at all.

To prevent defects, we have to understand the present symptoms that give us clues before defects actually occur. We must learn to recognize abnormal equipment conditions that can affect quality, the ones that give the vague impression that the machine is acting strangely. Only then can we hope to achieve zero defects.

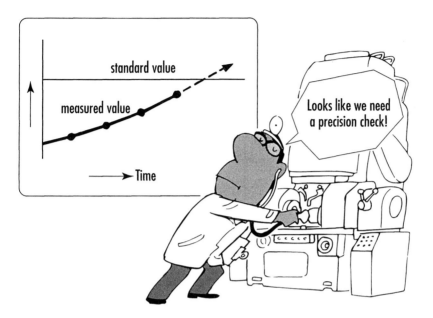

What Is Quality Maintenance?

One extremely effective way to achieve zero defects is to develop a "quality maintenance" program in which we first set up equipment so defects don't occur and then manage it properly to maintain that condition.

Quality maintenance means figuring out the equipment conditions in which defects won't occur, setting them up as the standards, monitoring and measuring actual equipment conditions over time, and confirming that the actual conditions are within the standard conditions. In this way, we can observe shifts in the measured values and foresee the possibility of defects. This lets us take action to prevent defects before they occur. The following sections explain some concepts and methods for applying this quality maintenance approach.

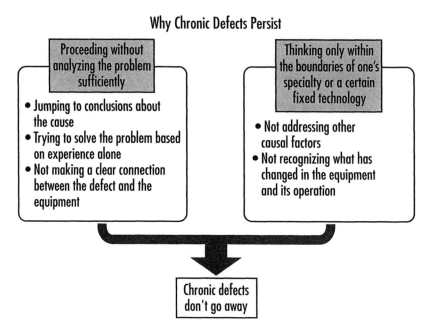

Why Chronic Defects Persist

Proceeding without analyzing the problem sufficiently
- Jumping to conclusions about the cause
- Trying to solve the problem based on experience alone
- Not making a clear connection between the defect and the equipment

Thinking only within the boundaries of one's specialty or a certain fixed technology
- Not addressing other causal factors
- Not recognizing what has changed in the equipment and its operation

Chronic defects don't go away

Sporadic Defects and Chronic Defects

Looking at the forms defects take, we can classify them as either *sporadic*—occurring suddenly and infrequently—or *chronic*—recurring over a long period.

We can usually deal with sporadic defects by restoring worn or failed parts to their proper states. Chronic defects, however, we often end up ignoring because our countermeasures don't make a difference. Yet these chronic defects can be a huge hindrance to raising productivity and equipment effectiveness, so combating them is extremely important.

The chart on this page lists some common reasons why we have trouble eliminating chronic defects.

Ideas for Reducing Chronic Defects	
Look beyond the obvious	• Don't worry too much about what has the most influence. • Think systematically and take measures against every abnormality
Review all factors carefully	• Think systematically about the form the defects took to understand what the factors are. • Give all the possible reasons for them.
Take abnormal conditions seriously	• Quantify the abnormality. • Use the inspection technology for your equipment to find signs of abnormal conditions.
Clarify the relationship between equipment and quality factors	• Determine the proper condition for each component to produce a quality result. • Manage the components according to those principles.
Monitor changes in the factors that need to be managed	• Understand changes over time through examination, measurement, and spot checks. • Determine treatment thresholds.

Ideas for Reducing Chronic Defects

If we want to eliminate chronic defects, it's important for us to understand the five ideas shown in the table above.

Look Beyond the Obvious

When we experience a defect rate of more than 2 or 3 percent, it's pretty easy to pin down the cause and effect relationships, and tackling the most obvious problem is usually the best way to proceed. But when the defect rate falls to 0.5 or 0.3 percent, we usually have multiple factors preventing us from achieving zero defects, and just concentrating on the obvious ones won't do the trick.

Instead of worrying about how much influence each factor has, we should think systematically and list all the factors we can come up with. Then we should investigate them thoroughly and determine how we will control each of them.

Review All Factors Carefully

When dealing with quality defect issues, we often decide which items to control before we have a clear picture of the relationship between defects and the state of the equipment. Much of the time, we overlook factors that may lead to defects or leave them off the list of items that need to be investigated.

It's no wonder that we can't reduce defects when we keep controlling the unimportant factors and not controlling the important factors. This happens because:

1. We don't have a clear grasp of the situation.

2. We've done a poor job of analyzing the factors.

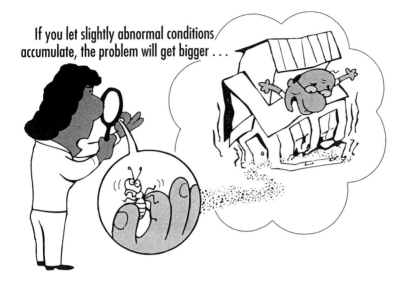

If you let slightly abnormal conditions accumulate, the problem will get bigger . . .

Take Abnormal Conditions Seriously

If we don't have our eyes trained to spot abnormal conditions or their symptoms, or if we don't take them seriously, we often just ignore them, and the defects they contribute to continue.

Furthermore, as mentioned earlier, our tendency to recognize only major malfunctions as problems prevents us from responding to slight abnormalities that can affect quality.

Slight abnormalities are small variances that make us wonder whether they're really flaws: bits of debris, or small amounts of play, wear, surface roughness, dirt, or vibration. In other words, they're the problems that we often overlook.

It's hard to tell just how much influence individual abnormalities have, but they can add up to throw the equipment out of its proper working order. That's why it's important not to overlook them and to use our senses to check for them.

109

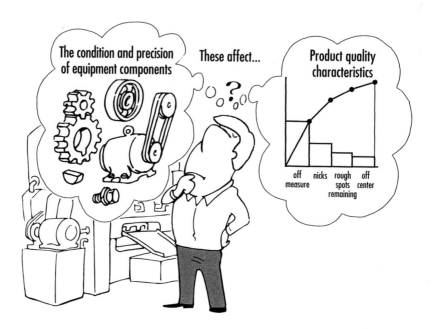

Clarify the Relationship Between Equipment and Quality Factors

110

People sometimes say, "Use the process to build in quality." In this age of mechanization and automation, however, this saying should be changed to, "Use the equipment to build in quality." The trouble is, the relationship between equipment conditions and product quality is often unclear to us.

To satisfy quality requirements, we must figure out the condition each equipment component must be in to guarantee quality and then manage the components according to those principles.

For example, we have to make firm standards for the precision of the components, parts, and assembly, and the static and dynamic precision, as well as determining the precision and rigidity of the attached standard surfaces. Once we've done this, it's important to maintain these standards strictly.

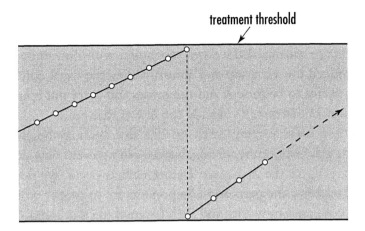

treatment threshold

Monitor Changes in the Factors
That Need to Be Managed

Even when we have a clear picture of the relationships between quality and the state of every component of our equipment, these factors more or less fluctuate with time. When this happens, we can't expect to achieve zero defects.

We can gain an idea of these changes over time through examination, measurement, and spot checks. Then we can determine the treatment threshold; that is, how much each factor can change before we must take action. This will allow us to prevent defects before they happen.

In other words, we need to check for all kinds of abnormalities. If there are abnormalities, we should monitor them again or else conduct a capability check, and then replace parts and fixtures as needed.

111

Basic Principles of Quality Maintenance

After we've measured the work machined with our equipment and noticed the variation and abnormalities, the usual course of action seems to be to seek out the causes and carry out countermeasures, but in fact, it's already too late at that point.

When we're playing catch-up like this, we may be able to prevent a defect from recurring, but we can't prevent new defects from arising in the first place. Before defects occur, we need to check whether the parts and components are in proper working order, confirm our results, and then fix anything that is out of the ordinary.

To make this possible, operators have to make autonomous maintenance a habit, so that they can:

1. Set standards for distinguishing normal and abnormal states.

2. Strictly follow all the standards and rules they have decided on.

3. Discover any abnormalities in the equipment that may cause defects.

4. Immediately begin the proper treatment for any abnormalities.

This is how operators can work with equipment to bring defects to zero.

Basic Principles of Quality Maintenance

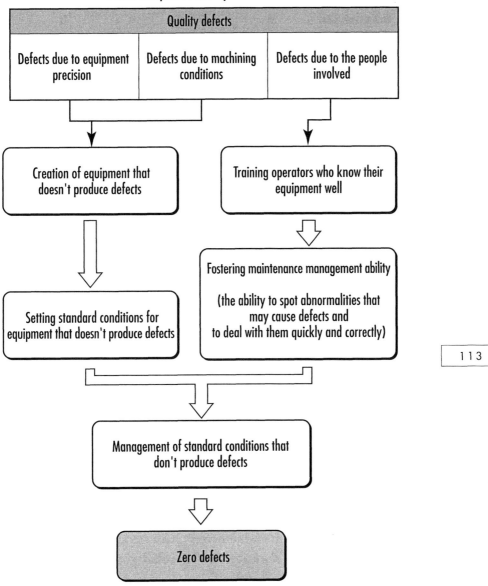

Inspection Checklist for Quality Characteristics				
Equipment part	**A**	**B**	**C**	**D**
Measurement items	Set position	Outer diameter vibrating Tip vibrating	Wear	Vibration
Standard values	$X = a$ $Y = b$	a or less b or less	c or less	d or less
Measurement interval	replacement, changeover	replacement, changeover	when starting operations	once a month
Quality characteristics				
Finished surface				
grinding traces	✓	✓	✓	
uneven shine	✓	✓		✓
rough spots	✓	✓		✓
Degree of concentricity	✓	✓		
Curvature	✓	✓	✓	
Nicks and scratches	✓		✓	

Setting Things Up So Defects Don't Occur

1. Take another look at the quality standards and quality characteristics of the products and processed items and make sure we understand them clearly. This lets us properly set up the equipment that machines and assembles the products and parts.

2. Keep detailed notes about when, where, and how any currently troublesome defects have occurred, then classify and rank them by the form they took and the part or component in which they occurred.

3. Get a clear picture of the structure of our equipment, the principles and standards of the process, the machining conditions, and the changeover methods.

4. Know the acceptable ranges for the static and dynamic precision of our equipment and the precision of the parts and fixtures.

The checklist shows an example of inspection points and values for a particular machining process.

Managing Conditions

Once we've set up our equipment so that defects won't occur, we have to manage it so that those conditions are firmly maintained and so that the various factors don't change beyond a certain limit.

When we see signs of change, we ought to shorten the interval between monitoring and measurements and take steps such as replacing parts when the treatment threshold is reached.

For example, if the vibration value has started to increase, or if a fixture is worn and is nearing its limit, or if there's a little bit of play, we can monitor the change through daily spot checks and do something about it at the right time. This will allow us to prevent defects before they occur.

Prepare a standard measurement surface.

Make inspections easier. Choose a measurement item that will lead you to all the other values.

By measuring vibration, you can check values that may indicate play, wear, or shaking.

Making Inspections Easier

The list of items that we need to check to keep defects from recurring can grow to an unmanageable size, even if we assign priorities to each item. This makes maintenance management difficult.

For this reason, we should identify the items that tend to vary and take steps to make them easier to maintain or improve them so they don't change. When there are items that we can't avoid checking, we should shorten the time required and cut down on the number of items to be checked.

For example, when checking the dynamic precision of a piece of equipment, we can make the inspection more efficient by measuring its vibration, which is easy to check and encompasses several inspection items. Since these inspections are carried out in the course of daily maintenance, it is important to have a clear idea of the control items, correct methods of inspection and measurement, ways to make measurement easier, standards for distinguishing normal from abnormal states, and measures to take when abnormalities appear.

The First Step: Completely Eliminating Accelerated Deterioration

An extremely effective method for implementing quality maintenance and making zero defects a reality is to use autonomous maintenance to root out accelerated deterioration. Indeed, this is the first step.

When autonomous maintenance is not firmly ingrained in operators' routines, breakdowns occur again and again. If we haven't cultivated the ability to recognize abnormalities, we cannot eliminate accelerated deterioration. Thus, even if we have set up conditions that are supposed to prevent defects, we will find it difficult to practice maintenance management correctly.

In addition, when breakdowns keep recurring, we may try to set up conditions that won't produce defects. But if we aren't strict enough in our analysis of the series of factors that causes malfunctions, it will be difficult for us to set up the proper conditions to eliminate them.

117

From Adjustment to Control

Another important thing to remember related to zero defects is that the very first product produced after changeover should be a high-quality item.

We may wonder why it's hard to achieve consistent quality right after changeover, but we can eliminate trial runs and adjustments if we remember to:

1. Keep the precision of our equipment at its proper level.

2. Keep the precision of the tools and fixtures at their proper level.

3. Have a clear picture of the parts that will serve as standards.

We need to change "adjustment" to "control."

Here, too, setting up the conditions is the key step. We can also review the principles set out in Chapter 3 to learn how to conduct a one-step defect-free changeover.

CHAPTER SUMMARY

Reliable product quality is a prerequisite for doing business today. As our plants become more sophisticated, automated, and energy efficient, much responsibility for quality shifts from people to machines. This motivates us to focus on equipment conditions to maintain product quality. To prevent defects, we have to understand the symptoms that give clues before defects actually occur.

A "quality maintenance" program is an effective way to achieve zero defects. Quality maintenance means figuring out the equipment conditions in which defects won't occur, setting them up as the standards, monitoring and measuring actual equipment conditions over time, and confirming that actual conditions are within the standards. This lets us observe shifts in measured values, foresee the possibility of defects, and take action to prevent them.

Defects are either *sporadic*—occurring suddenly and infrequently—or *chronic*—recurring over a long period. Chronic defects are often ignored because our actions don't make a difference. But they do reduce productivity, quality, and equipment effectiveness. To deal with chronic defects, we must look beyond the obvious causes to think systematically and list all possible factors, then investigate them thoroughly and determine how we will control each of them.

Our tendency to recognize only major malfunctions as problems prevents us from responding to slight abnormalities that can affect quality. Slight abnormalities are small variances that we often overlook: bits of debris, or small amounts of play, wear, surface roughness, dirt, or vibration.

Next, we must figure out the condition each equipment component must be in to guarantee quality and then manage the components according to those principles. Finally, we must monitor changes in the factors that need to be managed, determining a treatment threshold when we will take action.

Tips for preventing defects:

1. Take another look at quality standards to be sure we understand them.

2. Keep detailed notes on all defect occurrences.

3. Get a clear picture of the equipment structure.

4. Know the acceptable ranges for static and dynamic precision.

Identify items that tend to vary and make them easier to maintain, or improve them so they don't vary. Simplify inspection by using a measure that can indicate problems in several items, then investigate further. Find ways to change setup adjustments into one-step control.

Additional Resources

Books and Learning Packages

Japan Institute of Plant Maintenance, ed., *Autonomous Maintenance for Operators* (Productivity Press, 1997). A Shopfloor Series book that supports autonomous maintenance with information on basic AM activities and team learning aids.

Japan Institute of Plant Maintenance, ed., *TPM for Every Operator* (Productivity Press, 1996). Explains TPM activities carried out by operators, including autonomous maintenance, focused improvement, and safety activities. Introduces the six big losses in easy-to-grasp terms.

Nachi-Fujikoshi Corporation, *Training for TPM* (Productivity Press, 1990). A classic case study from a world-class machine tool company that won the PM Prize for maintenance excellence. Includes unique information on focused improvement and P-M analysis.

Productivity Press Development Team, *5S for Operators* and *5S for Operators Learning Package* (Productivity Press, 1996). Introduces operators to the 5S system for workplace organization, cleaning, and standardization—the foundation for TPM and other advanced improvement approaches. Learning Package includes leader's discussion guide, overheads, color slides of examples, and resource books.

Productivity Press Development Team, *TPM for Every Operator Learning Package* (Productivity Press, 1997). Provides a framework for group learning about TPM and autonomous maintenance basics, as well as application exercises to see how TPM concepts might apply in the learners' work areas. Includes leader's discussion guide and overheads, study guides for participants, and exercise worksheets.

K. Shirose, *TPM for Workshop Leaders* (Productivity Press, 1992). Describes the hands-on leadership issues of TPM implementation for shopfloor TPM team leaders, with case studies and practical examples to help support autonomous maintenance activities.

K. Shirose, et al., *P-M Analysis* (Productivity Press, 1995). An advanced TPM approach for eliminating chronic defects and failures due to subtle or complex causes.

K. Shirose, ed., *TPM for Supervisors* (Productivity Press, 1996). Presents the basic methodology of TPM, with a focus on operator activities to reduce equipment-related losses and maximize equipment effectiveness.

K. Shirose, ed., *TPM Team Guide* (Productivity Press, 1996). A Shopfloor Series book that teaches how to lead TPM team activities in the workplace and develop effective presentations of project results.

K. Suehiro, *Eliminating Minor Stoppages on Automated Equipment* (Productivity Press, 1992). Presents a method for increasing performance by treating minor stoppages that reduce the productivity of automated equipment.

S. Tsuchiya, *Quality Maintenance* (Productivity Press, 1992). Describes an equipment maintenance approach specifically for preventing product quality losses.

Training and Consulting

The Productivity Consulting Group delivers hands-on public events and customized in-house training and consulting for TPM implementation. Telephone: 1-800-966-5423.

About the Editor

The Japan Institute of Plant Maintenance is a nonprofit research, consulting, and educational organization that helps companies increase organizational efficiency and profitability through improved maintenance of manufacturing equipment, processes, and facilities. JIPM is the sponsoring organization for the PM Prize, awarded annually to recognize excellence in companywide maintenance systems. Based in Japan, JIPM is the innovator of methodologies that have been implemented around the world. Productivity Press is pleased to be the publisher of the English editions of many groundbreaking JIPM publications.